AF480325

This book belongs to:

____

Daddy and the Sugar Monster
By Erica N. Cole

Published by
Erica N. Cole

Daddy and the Sugar Monster

Daddy and the Sugar Monster

By Erica N. Cole

I have a parent that has to fight

a sugar monster EVERYDAY,

and I call him DADDY.

I was five years old

when I learned

daddy was sick.

One day, daddy would not wake up from sleeping.

I was scared and began to cry.

I called my mommy and she said, "Everything will be okay."

Mommy called 9-1-1 for help. I heard loud sirens.

It was a big truck with flashing lights!

Daddy had to go the hospital.

I did not know what was going on.

I asked my mommy, "What happened to daddy?"

She said, "Your daddy has diabetes."

"Diabetes?" I said.

Mommy said, "Yes, diabetes. It's when an organ called a pancreas fails to produce insulin in your body. Insulin helps regulate blood sugar levels. So, a bad pancreas equals diabetes."

I was sad because I wanted daddy to have a good pancreas.

Mommy said that sugar diabetes could be a monster sometimes.

I asked, "Daddy is fighting a sugar monster?"

She said, "Yes baby, daddy has been fighting with the sugar monster for a long time."

I imagined daddy fighting this huge scary monster everyday but at the end, daddy won the fight!

The doctor came out and told us that they were able to get my daddy's blood sugar to a normal level.

So, that meant that daddy could come back home.

MEDS

We made it back home.

Daddy looked tired.

I asked him if he was okay.

He said, "Yes, honey I'm okay. Can you bring daddy his special bag, please?"

Daddy kept medicine in his special bag.

He said that the medicine made him

feel better.

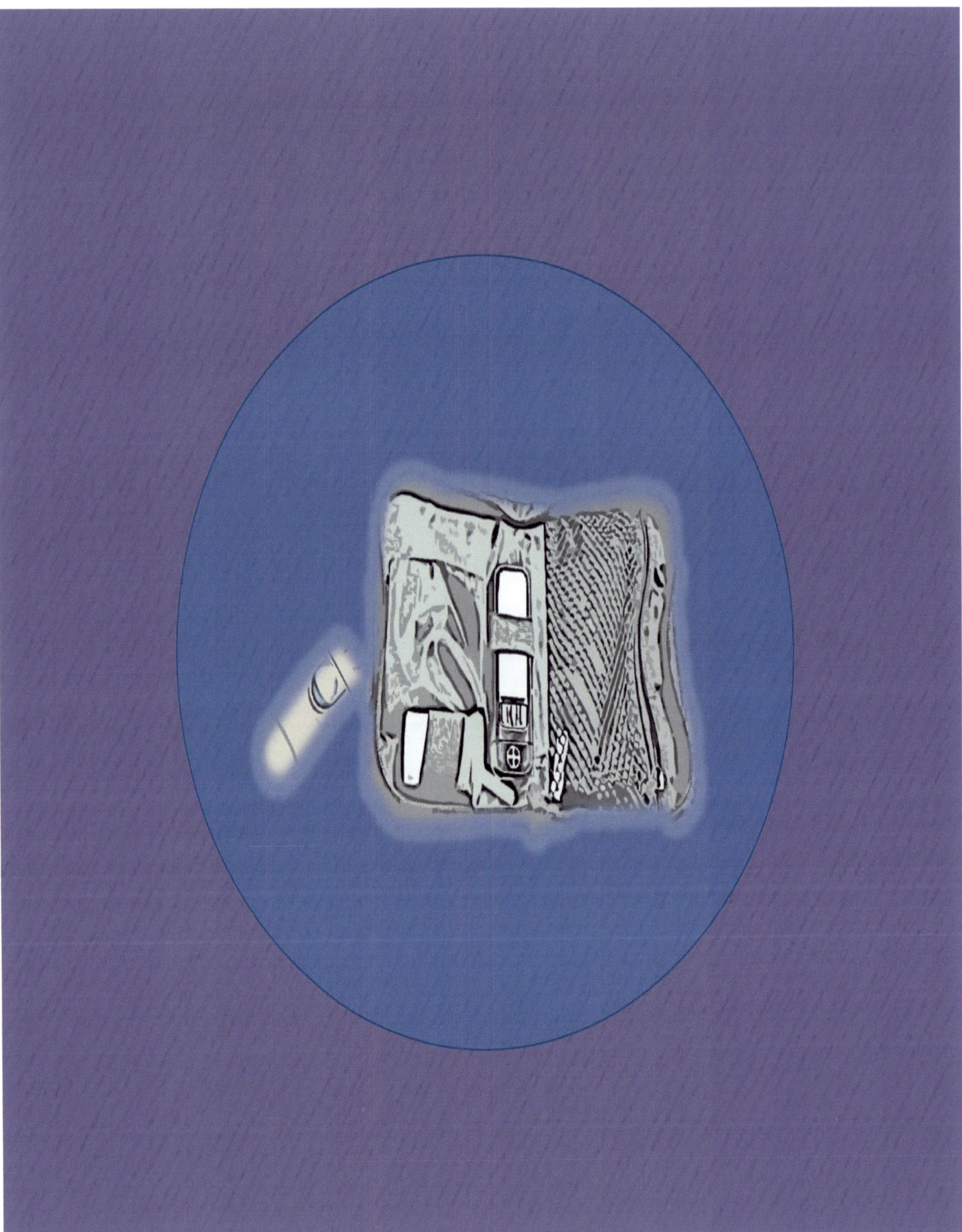

I saw daddy eat a snack and reach for his pouch.

Inside was a small needle, a monitor, and a tube of white strips.

The monitor lets daddy know when his sugar levels are high or low.

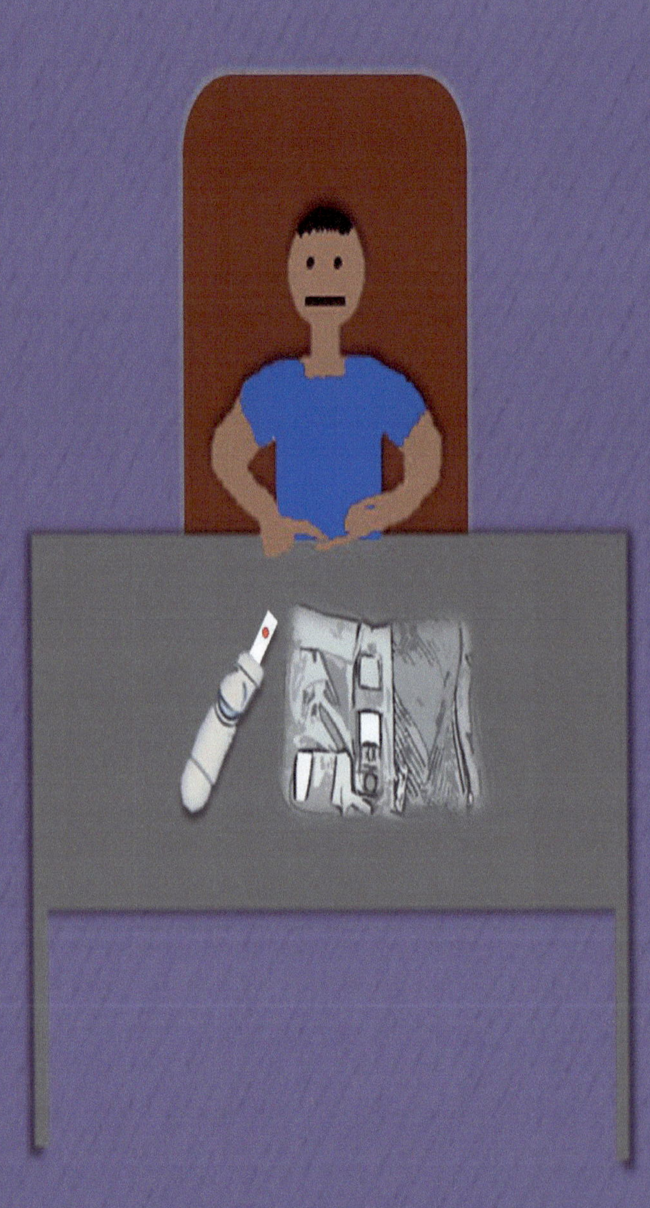

He put the white strip inside the monitor.

And, then he stuck his finger with the needle to put blood on the white strip.

The monitor will let daddy know how much insulin he will need throughout the night.

I did not like seeing daddy stick himself with that little needle.

I asked my mommy, "Will daddy have to do this forever?"

She said, "Yes baby, because there is no cure for diabetes. But your daddy can live well if he eats right, exercises, and takes his medicine daily."

Although, daddy would still have to

fight the sugar monster,

I was happy to know that daddy

would be with me for a long time!

This book is dedicated to my daddy!